P9-CRI-800

You and

RELATIVITY

Mary Lou Clark, a teacher of chemistry and physics, finds young minds eager and able to grasp ideas that may seem difficult to an adult.

She begins with a relatively simple answer to the question: What is up? She establishes the importance of one's "frame of reference" and then goes on, step by step, to some of the more complex concepts of Einstein's Theory of Relativity.

There is no absolute motion.
There is no absolute time.
Light always moves through
space at the same speed.
Length shortens with speed.
Mass increases with velocity.

Profound ideas that seem to violate common sense can be exciting.

Mrs. Clark had some good help with this book at a national conference of teachers of physics who were most pleased with it and surprised that she could present her subject so simply and without mathematics.

AND

RELATIVITY

By Mary Lou Clark, M.S.
Illustrations by
Bill Sanders

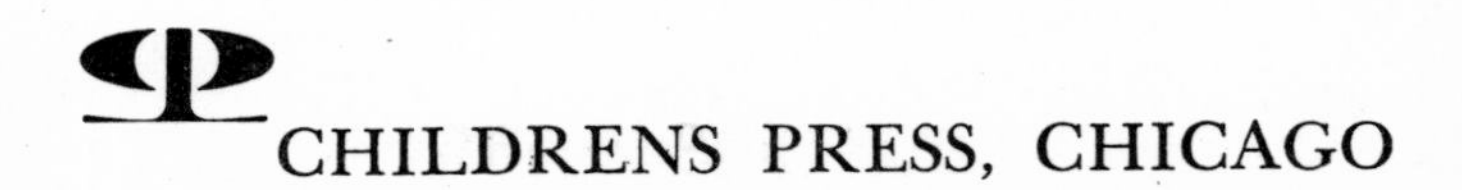

Library of Congress Catalog Card Number: 6512214

 Printed in the U.S.A.
Published simultaneously in Canada

2 3 4 5 6 7 8 9 10 11 12 13 14 15 16 17 18 19 20 21 22 23 24 25 R 75 74 73 72 71 70 69 68 67 66

ABOUT THE AUTHOR

Mary Lou Clark is a teacher of chemistry and physics at Ligonier Valley Senior High School. She has B.S. and M.S. degrees from the University of Pittsburgh and is working for a master's degree in physics at Carnegie Institute of Technology.

The Clarks live on a 160 acre farm where their four children have become skilled horsemen and where they can walk under the open sky to learn astronomy.

The children go off to school every morning with their mother who teaches and writes with the assurance that the young mind is eager to learn and able to tackle subjects difficult for adults.

ABOUT THE ARTIST

Bill Sanders is a young, professional artist, graduate of Illinois University, and now associated with an art studio in Chicago. He and his wife, who is an artist, too, live in an old coach house in Evanston.

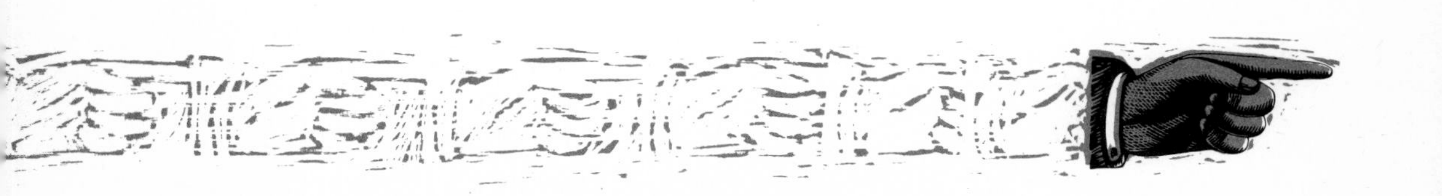

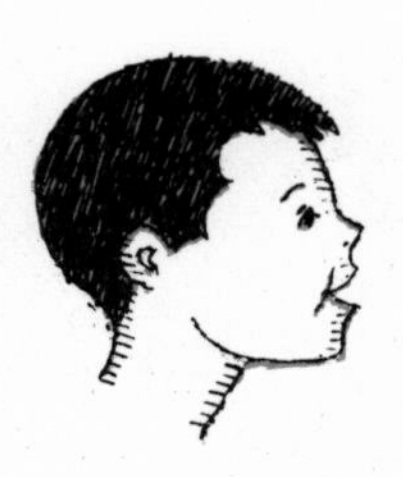

You and Relativity

What is up?

What is down?

That is easy you say. When I throw a ball into the air, it goes up; then it comes down. If I look at the sky, I look up. When I drop something, it falls down.

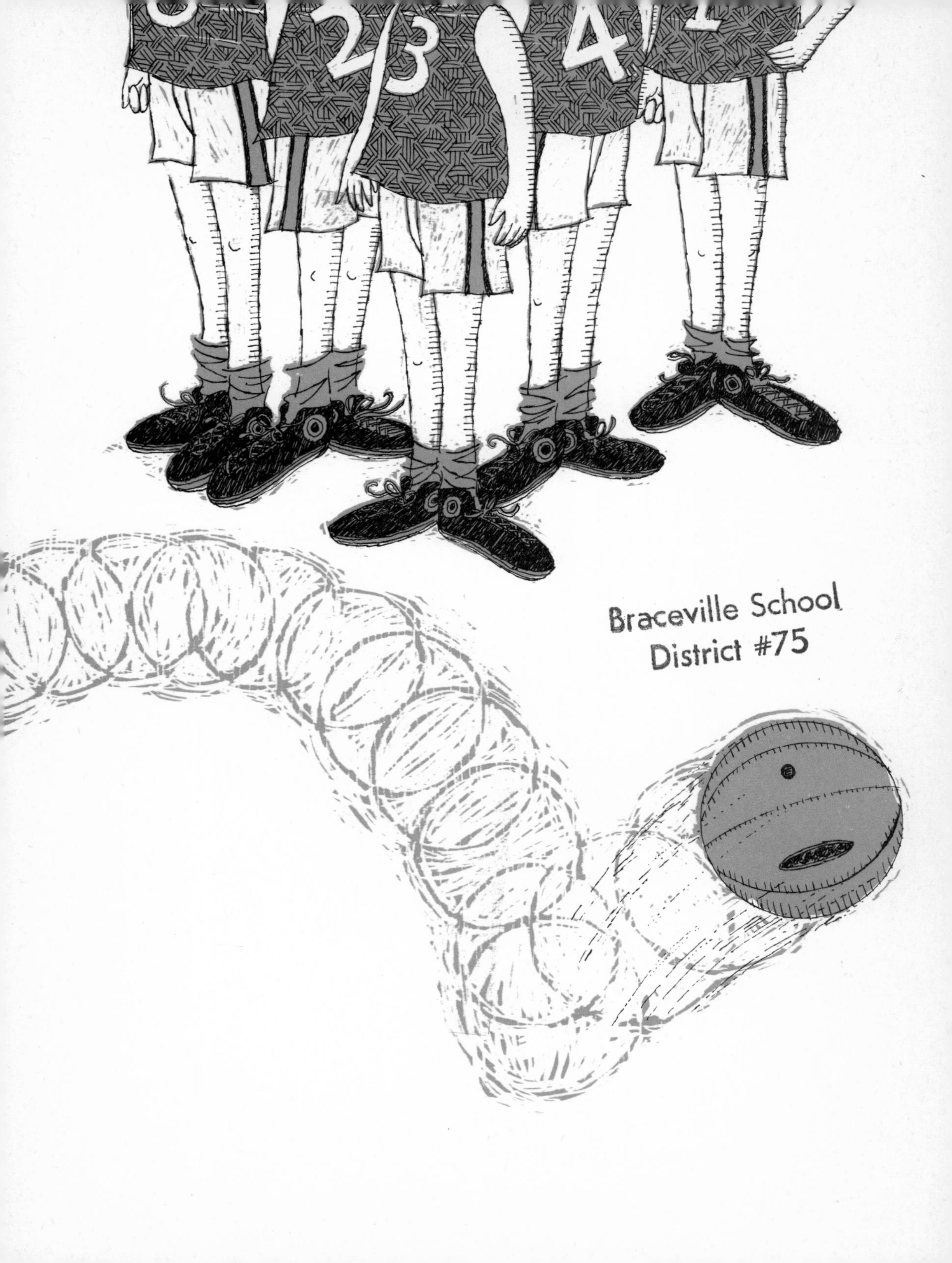
2
3
4

Now think about this. If several people want to go to the third floor of a building, will they all go up? It depends on where they are when they start. Mr. X, who is on the first floor, will go up to get to the third floor. Mr. Y, who is on the sixth floor, must go down to get to the third floor. *Relative* to the first floor, the third floor is up, but *relative* to the sixth floor, the third floor is down. The matter of up and down depends on where you are. It depends on your *frame of reference.*

DINING ROOMS
MENU

Let's try a thought experiment. A thought experiment is an experiment that you must think about only, because you can not really do it. Great scientists do a lot of thought experiments. They are fun. Doing a thought experiment is like playing make-believe.

Suppose you could make a hole right through the center of the earth and see the people on the other side. How would they look to you? To you they would be upside down. If the imaginary hole had a glass cover over it to stop the people from falling through, you would see the bottoms of their shoes as they walked across the glass. If they looked through the hole, you would be upside down to them. *Relative* to you

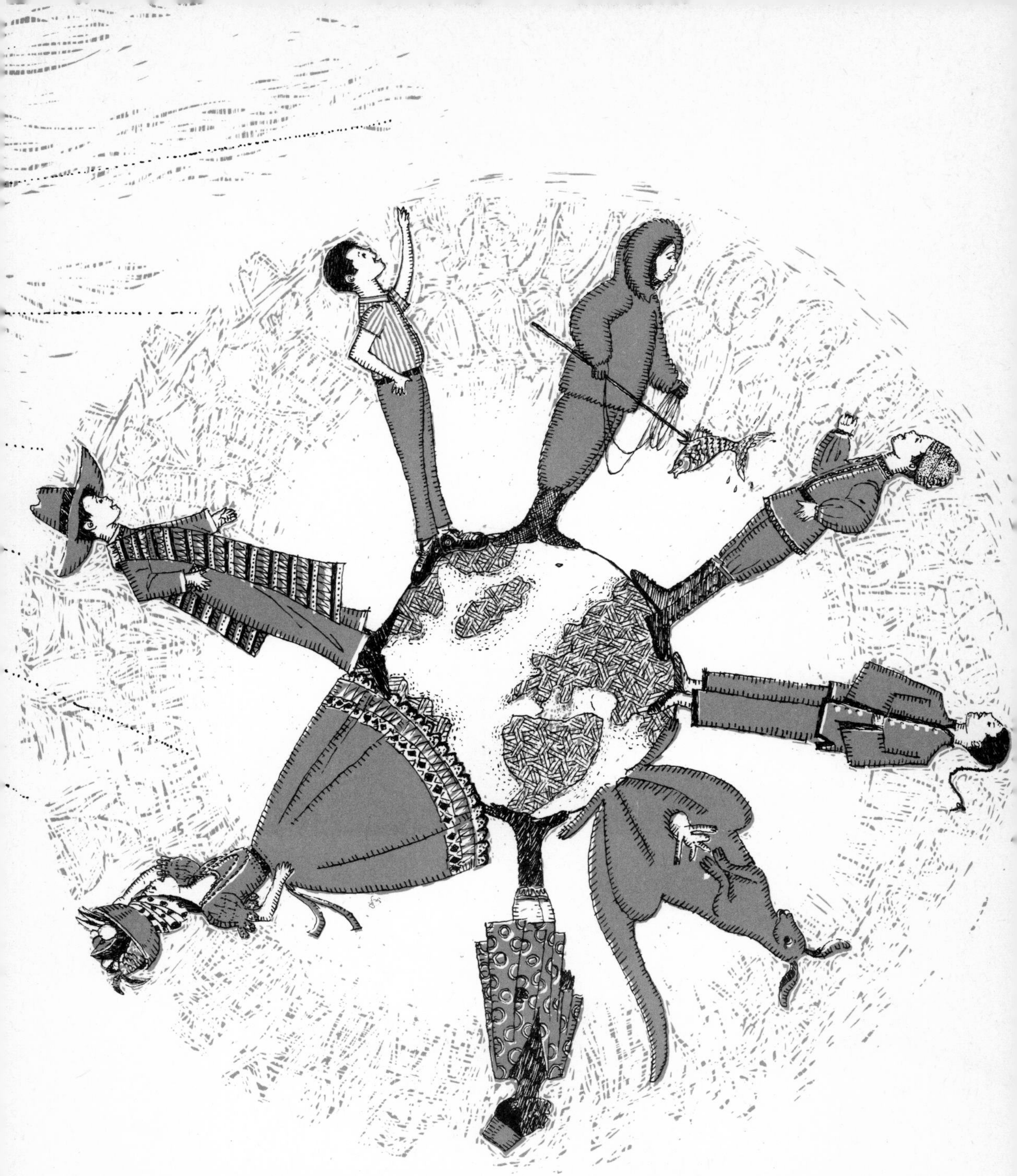

they are upside down. *Relative* to them you are upside down. It depends on your frame of reference.

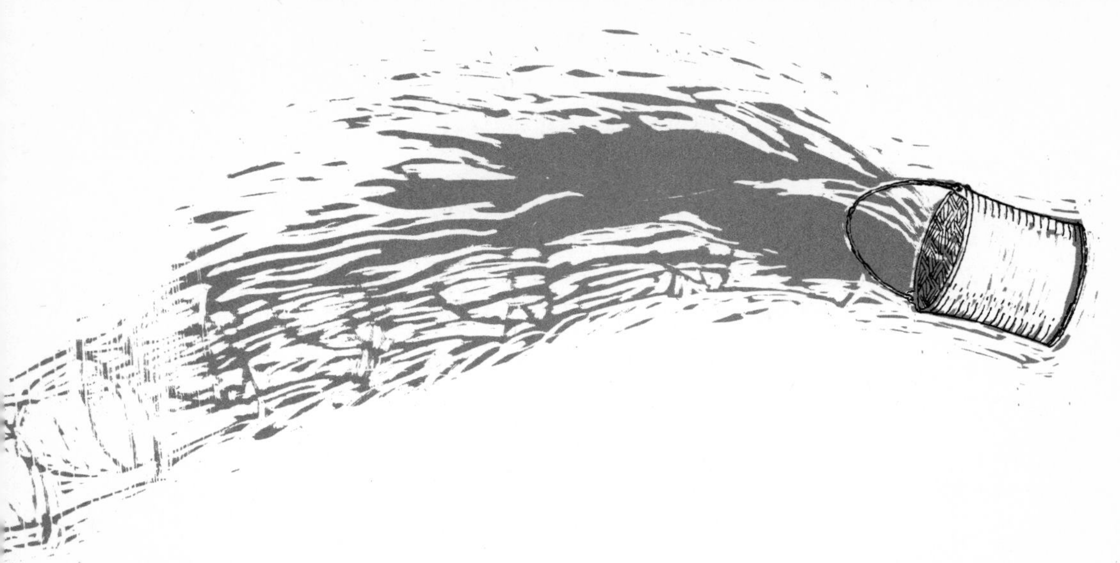

On our planet earth, down is toward the center of the earth. Up means away from the earth.

The earth's attraction for objects is called the *force of gravity.* When an object is dropped, it is pulled to the earth by the force of gravity. Sometimes a force is created that is greater than the force of gravity.

To prove this put some water into a bucket and take it outdoors. Now swing the bucket rapidly in a vertical circle—a curved path circling the direction from your knees to your head and back to your knees. The water will remain in the bottom of the bucket as long as you keep swinging the bucket rapidly in a circle. In swinging the bucket a new force is created. This force is called *centrifugal force.* (We pronounce it sen-TRIF-yuh-guhl.)

As you swing the bucket centrifugal force becomes *greater* than the force of gravity. This forms a false force of gravity. The water pushes hard against the bottom of the bucket. The water stays in the bucket even when the bucket is upside down. When you stop swinging the bucket on its circular path, centrifugal force is halted and the force of gravity takes over. If you were to let go of the bucket while swinging it, the bucket would fly away tangent to the circle.

Pretend you are on a spaceship. It is shaped like a huge doughnut. As it whirls through space, a centrifugal force is created. The strong centrifugal force forms a gravity field. This false gravity field allows the people in the ship to use the outer rim of the ship as a floor. They can walk along the outer rim of the ship. Objects they drop fall to the "floor." While they are traveling in this ship, up becomes "toward the center" of the ship and down means "away from" the ship.

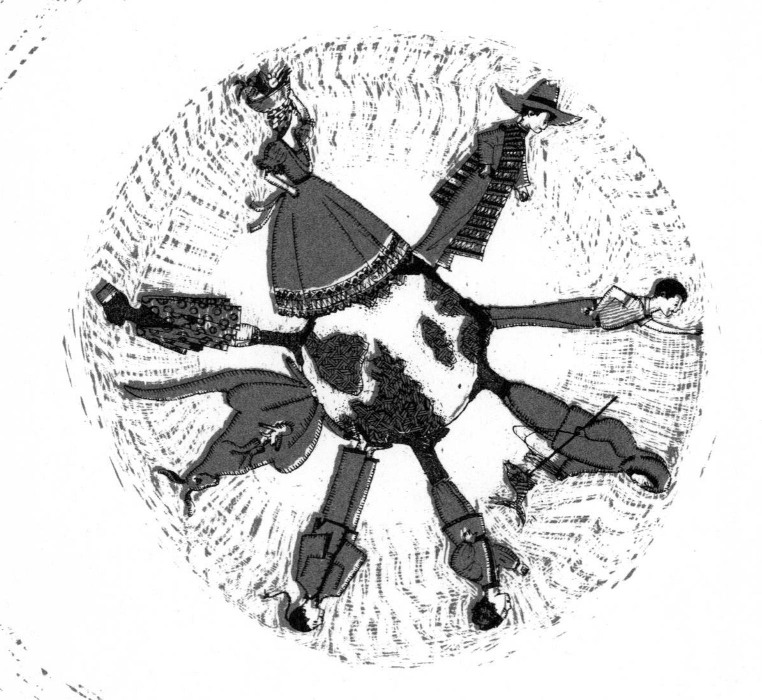

How does this compare to the meaning of up and down on planet earth?

Up and down are not the only directions that are relative. What do you think about left and right? Are they always the same to everybody? If you are not sure about the answers to these questions, do this experiment:

Stand face to face with another person. Now each of you move one step to the right. Did you both move in the same direction?

What happens if two people stand back-to-back and each one walks forward?

How are the directions north, east, south, and west relative depending on the frame of reference?

Forward, backward, inward, outward
Left or right—which place?
Relatively speaking
There's no up and down in space.

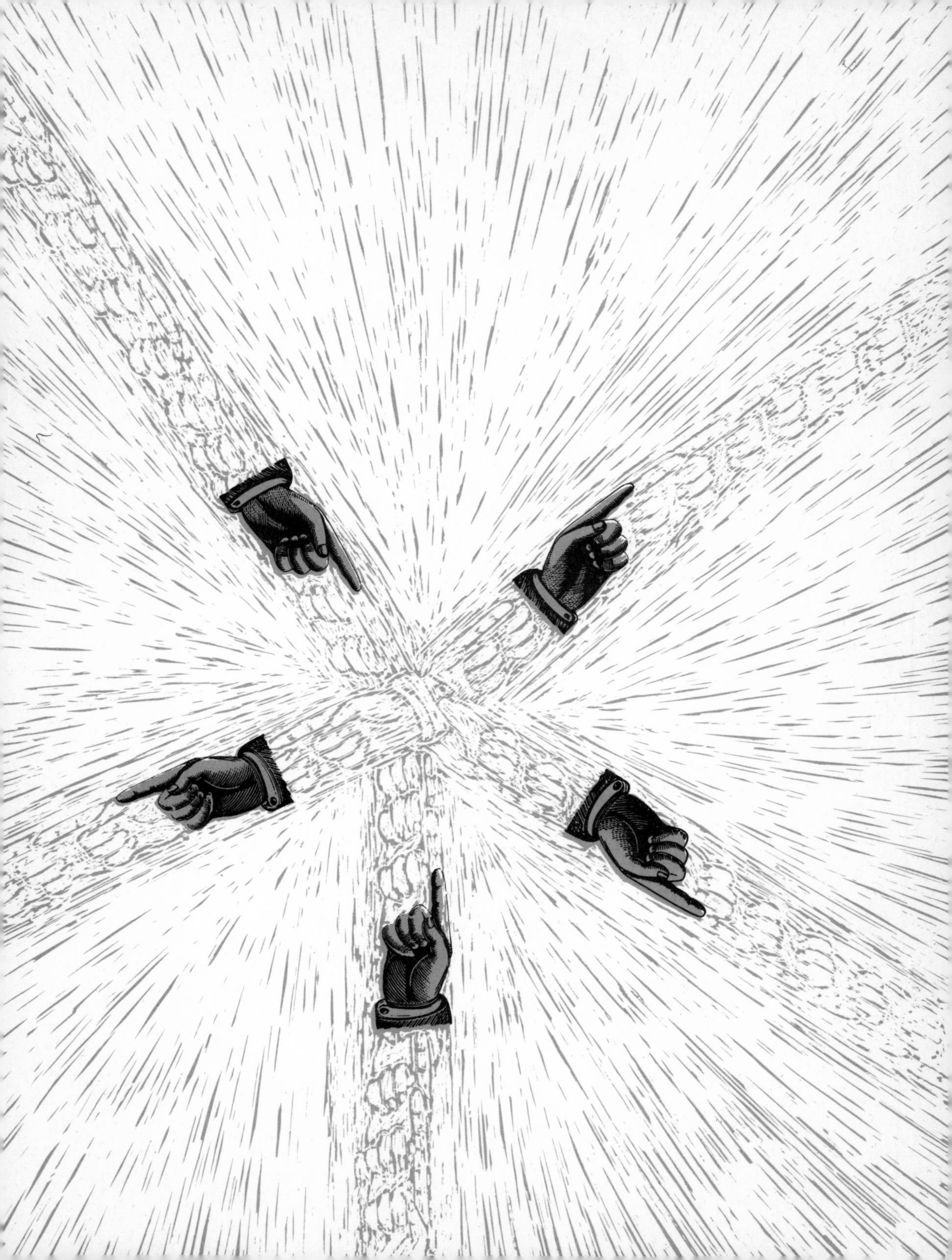

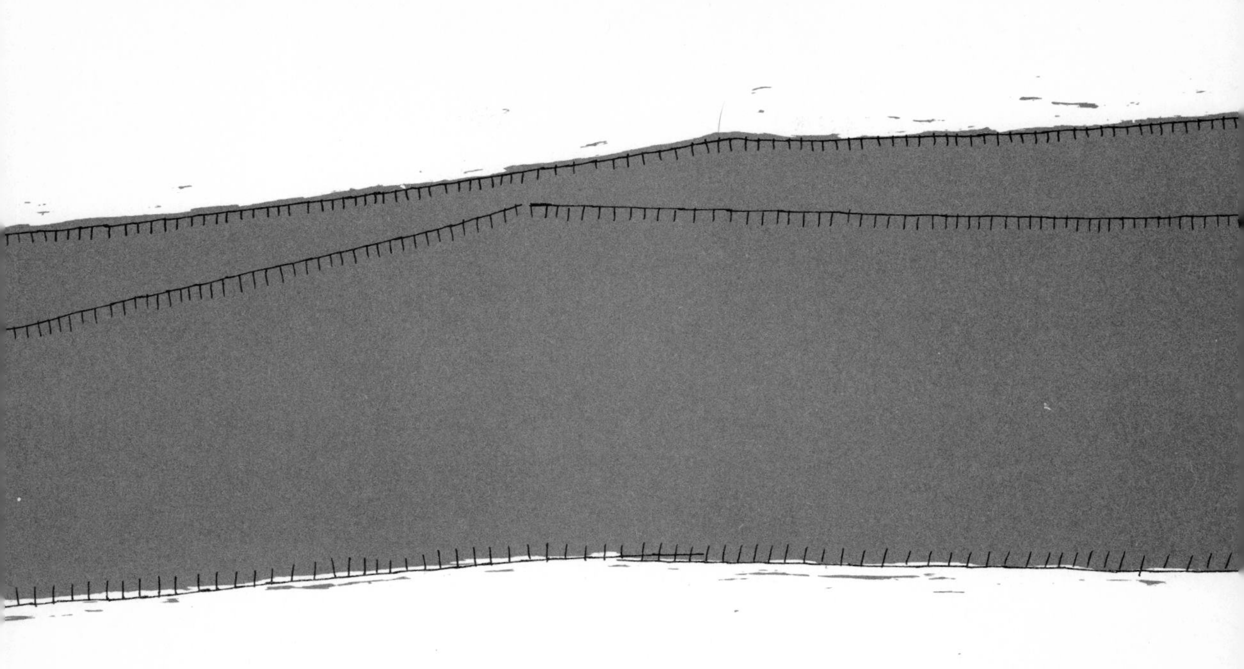

When Gulliver traveled to the land of Lilliput, he was a giant compared to those tiny people. If by some strange happening Gulliver became the same size as the Lilliputians, then what would be expected? Would Gulliver think he was smaller than he had been? Would there be a way for Gulliver to tell he was not his normal size?

This brings up another thought experiment. Suppose the same thing happened to you while you slept. During the night everything became smaller than it was when you went to sleep—you, your bed, your room, your house. This is not a case of the EAT ME cakes and DRINK ME potions of *Alice in Wonderland* that kept Alice changing her size *relative to her surroundings.* Here is a situation in which *every single thing* changes—from atoms and molecules to the earth and sun.

How, then, could you tell that a change had taken place? There is no possible way. Since *everything* has grown smaller, there is nothing to use as a comparison. Everything is in the same proportion as it was before. You could not tell that you were smaller.

You could not measure yourself because the yardsticks have become smaller. We measure objects by comparing them to something else. From this thought experiment, we conclude that size, too, is relative.

Time, also, is relative. There is no absolute time. One period of time is measured by comparing it with another period of time. A year on earth is 365 days. This is the length of time for the earth to make one revolution around the sun. One year on Mercury is equal to 88 earth days. One year on Uranus is about 84 earth years. What makes a day? A day on earth is the period of the earth's turning on its axis. It is divided into hours, minutes and seconds.

Does ten years seem like a long time to you? A geologist who measures the age of the earth by fossil stories, thinks of ten years as a very short time. To a small child even tomorrow seems a long way off. A year at your present age seems shorter than it did when you were five years old.

As your clock strikes noon, is it noon for everybody? When you have the season of winter, is everybody having winter? As long as we are on earth our clocks are set by earth time and corrections can be made for the time zones. In space, time has a different frame of reference. Think about this. If there were no motion would time mean anything to us? Time depends on motion.

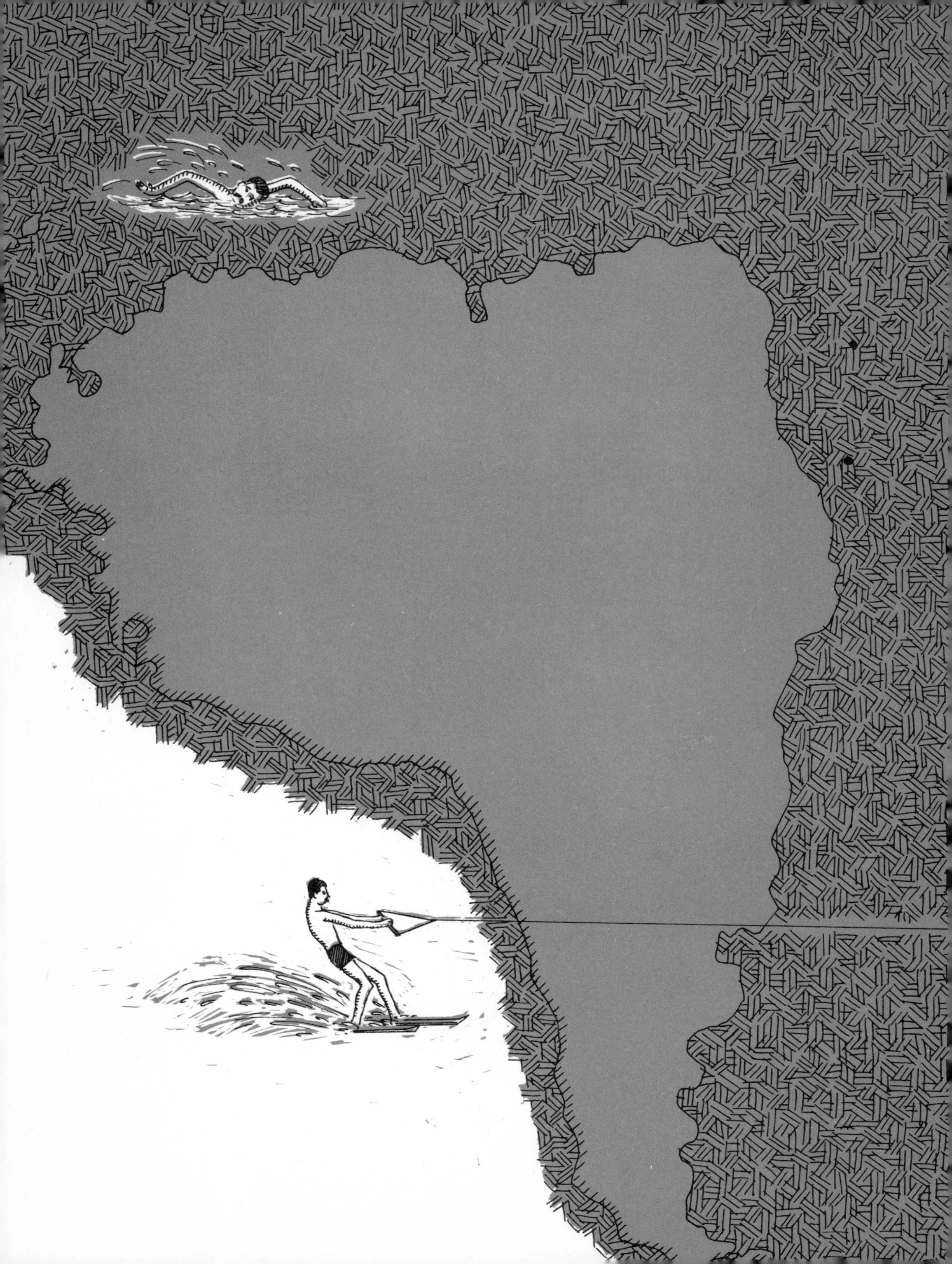

We have discussed direction, size, and time, all of which are relative. None of these are absolute. Surely something in this world must be absolute. Are all things relative depending on the frame of reference?

In this strange world of relativity what are your ideas about motion? Is motion absolute or is it relative? How can we prove that a body is moving or standing still? We have seen that direction, size, and time require a standard of comparison. Does motion, also, need a standard of comparison?

To find the answers to these questions, ride in a car moving smoothly at a constant speed. Close your eyes. Unless the road is bumpy or your body is swayed around a curve, you cannot

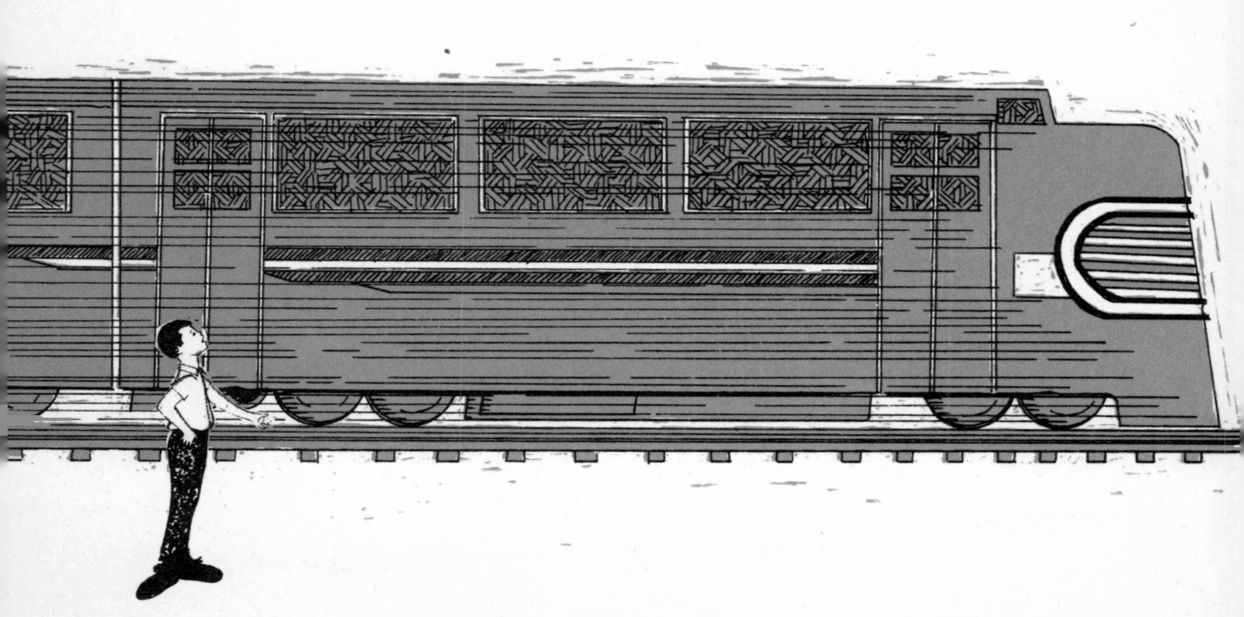

tell that you are moving. If the car had no windows and your eyes were open, you could not tell you were moving. The other people in the car would not appear to be moving. What would happen if you dropped an object? It would fall to the floor. This would be as normal as if you were sitting in a parked car. Unless you see the landscape passing by or are given clues by a bumpy or curving ride, you can not tell that you are in motion.

If you are riding in a smoothly running train and are traveling at 100 miles per hour and another train beside you is going at the same speed, it seems to you that you are standing still. If your train passes another train going 80 miles per hour in the opposite direction, your train seems to be going faster than 100 miles per hour. If you pass a train going 80 miles per hour in the same direction your train is going, then your train seems to be going slower than 100 miles per hour.

The train's speed of 100 miles per hour can be thought about in another way. Can you honestly say that 100 miles per hour is the true speed of the train? Why not?

The earth turns on its axis as it travels about 18 miles per second on its path around the sun. The sun itself hurtles through our galaxy, the Milky Way. The Milky Way moves through space relative to other galaxies. Add these to the train's speed of 100 miles per hour and you'll discover that you are traveling several thousand miles per hour!

Since it all depends on your frame of reference, we conclude that motion is relative. If you were in a spaceship and saw nothing passing by, you could not tell you were moving.

This is not where the story of relativity ends. This is only the beginning. The theory of relativity is very difficult to understand. The relativity theory can be understood completely only by mathematical equations. Without using the formulas only some of the facts and conclusions can be stated.
They can not be proved here.

Professor Albert Einstein (1879–1955) developed his Theory of Relativity by thinking about questions just like the ones that have been asked of you in this book. His Theory of Relativity is made up of two parts. One is the Special Theory of Relativity formed in 1905 and the other is his General Theory of Relativity put forth in 1915. The Special Theory makes use of the speed of light—186,000 miles per second. The General Theory explains the effects produced when an object in motion changes its path or velocity.

In 1887 two American scientists, Albert Michelson and Edward Morley, performed an experiment that paved the way for Einstein's theory. By comparing accurately the speed of light in one direction with light's speed in another direction through reflections on an arrangement of mirrors, the Michelson-Morley experiment disproved the long-existing "ether-drag" theory.

Scientists knew that light traveled in waves. They thought that light waves must travel through something in much the same way that waves travel through water. Without the water there would be no waves. Physicists up to this time believed that all space was filled with a substance through which light traveled. They called this substance *ether.*

The ether-drag theory said this: As the earth went around the sun at 18 miles per second, it would create an ether wind of 18 miles per second. The speed of light measured from one direction would be slower than the speed of light measured from the other direction. Light would be slowed down or "dragged" as it came through the ether wind. The Michelson-Morley experiment proved that it made no difference from which direction light was measured. Therefore, there was no ether in space.

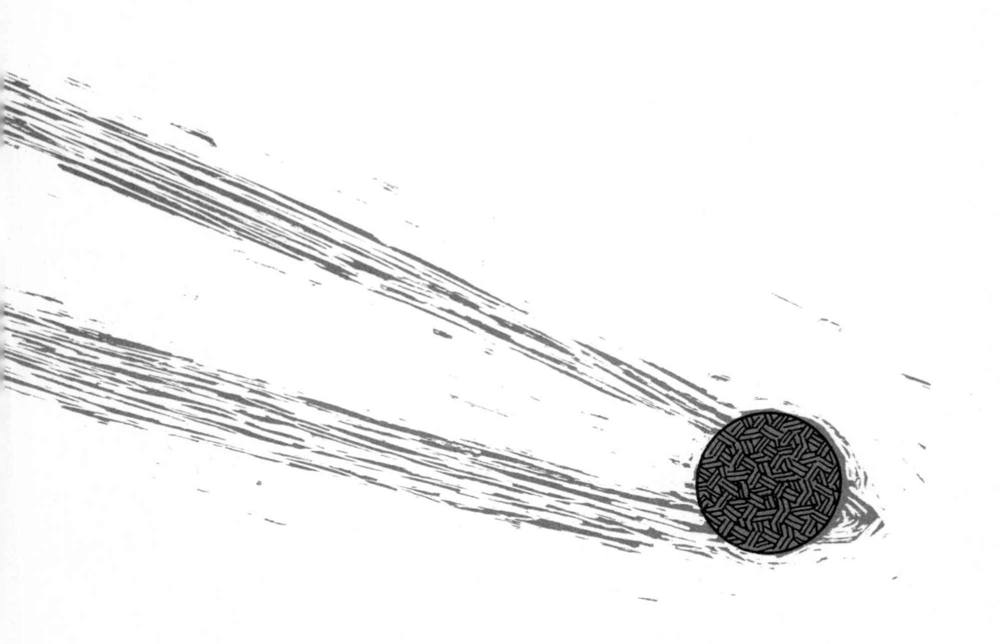

This is what the Special Theory of Relativity tells us. Regardless of how a space traveler moves relative to the source of a beam of light—whether he is moving beside it, away from it, or toward it—he will always get the same speed for the light—186,000 miles per second. (Remember what was said about the 100-mile-per-hour train.) Here at last is an absolute measurement. The speed of light relative to the person observing it always remains the same.

Another part of Einstein's theory tells us that the length of a body shortens with speed. As an object approaches the speed of light, an observer will measure the object to be shorter than it really is. The object appears to shorten its length in the direction in which it is going. According to the theory the object would disappear if it traveled at the speed of light—186,000 miles per second. This does not mean that the matter making up the body would disappear. It means that the body would be going so fast that no one could see it. No object can move faster than the speed of light. If it could it would return before it started. Then there would be two of them!

There once was a lady named Bright
Who could travel much faster than light;
She left one day in a relative way
And came back the previous night!

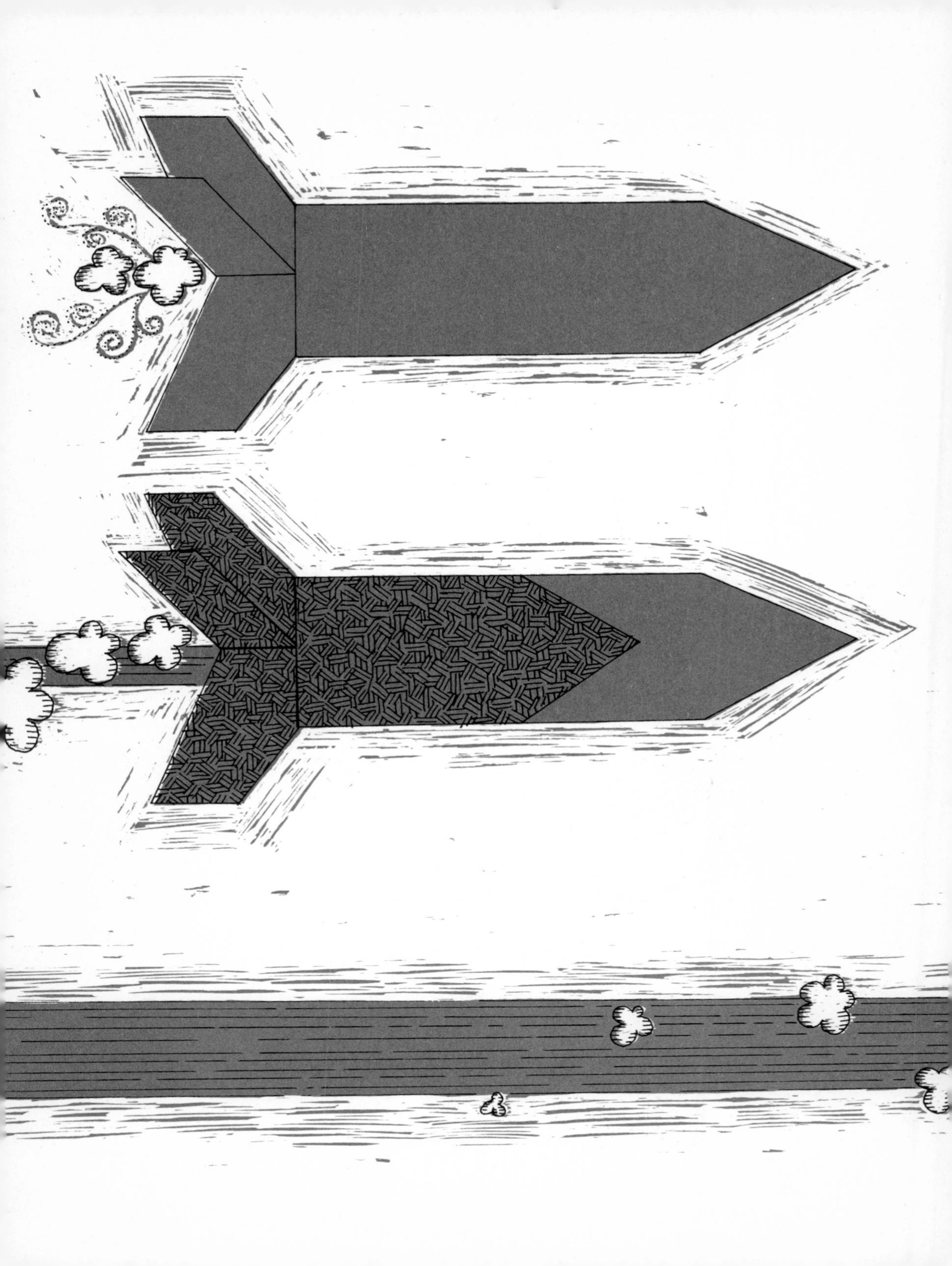

Watch the cars of a speeding train passing by. Don't they seem shorter than when at rest? You can notice a shortening effect on the broken lines painted on the highway as your car whizzes past them. This is not relativity but only an optical illusion that helps to explain the contraction effect. To have the contraction effect take place an object must be traveling near the speed of light. Then the person observing the object would measure it to be shorter than it really was.

This idea of an object shortening its length in the direction in which it is moving was first mentioned by an Irish physicist, George Francis Fitzgerald, and a Dutch physicist, Hendrik Antoon Lorentz. This part of the relativity theory is still called the Lorentz-Fitzgerald contraction.

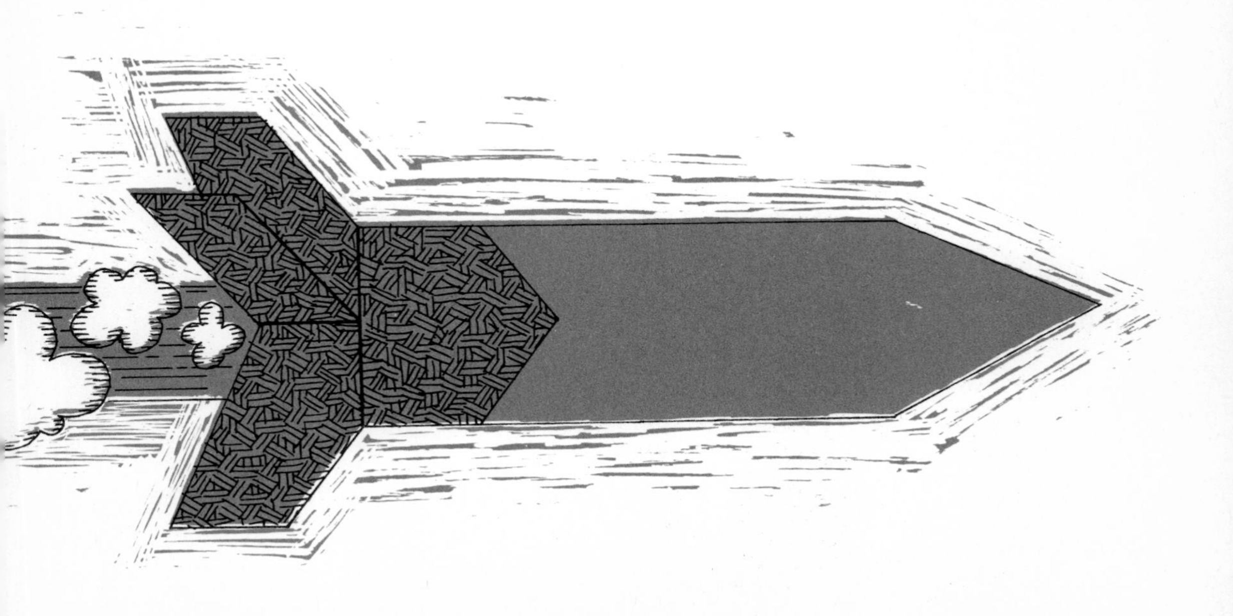

"The mass of an object increases with its velocity" is another statement in Einstein's theory. When you hold a baseball in your hand, it doesn't seem to weigh very much. However, when you catch one that has been well hit by the bat, its weight increases a lot. This is not relativity but is an example to help you understand this part of the theory. The baseball would have to be going near the speed of light for this relativistic mass effect to be measured.

12
1
2
3
4
5
6
7
8
9
10
11

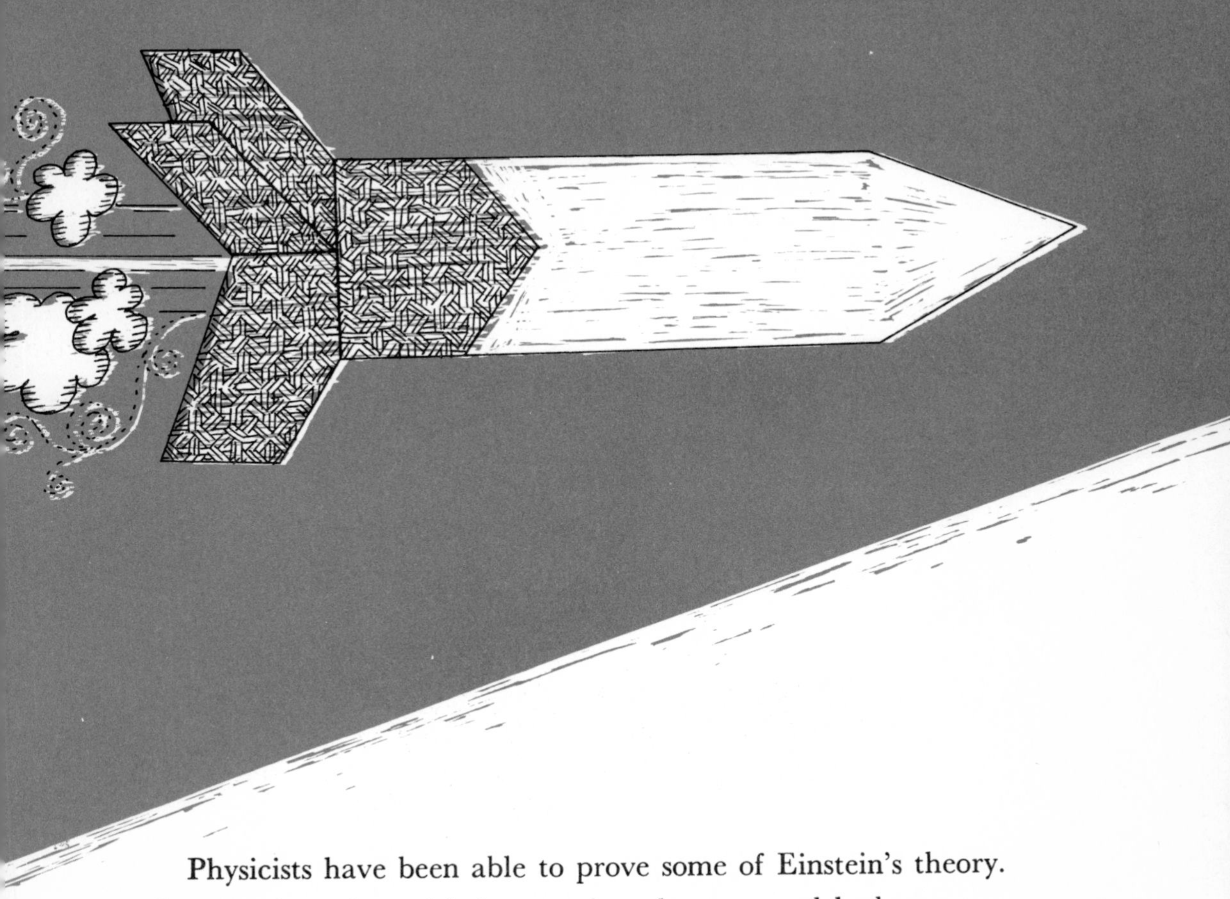

Physicists have been able to prove some of Einstein's theory. By experimenting with fast-moving electrons and hydrogen atoms, they have proven that time slows down and mass increases with velocity. In 1958 Rudolf Mossbauer discovered the "Mossbauer effect" which proved Einstein's prediction that time is slowed down by gravity.

Einstein's theory tells us:

1. There is no absolute time.
2. There is no absolute motion.
3. Light always moves through space at the same speed.
4. Length shortens with speed.
5. Mass increases with velocity.

The ideas presented in the Theory of Relativity are profound. They appear to violate common sense. If we had a very powerful telescope and could look at the earth from the sun, we would see things that happened eight minutes ago. Using the super telescope and viewing earth from a celestial body much farther away than the sun, we would see World War II, World War I, or even the Civil War. Our sights would be set on history. Incredible!

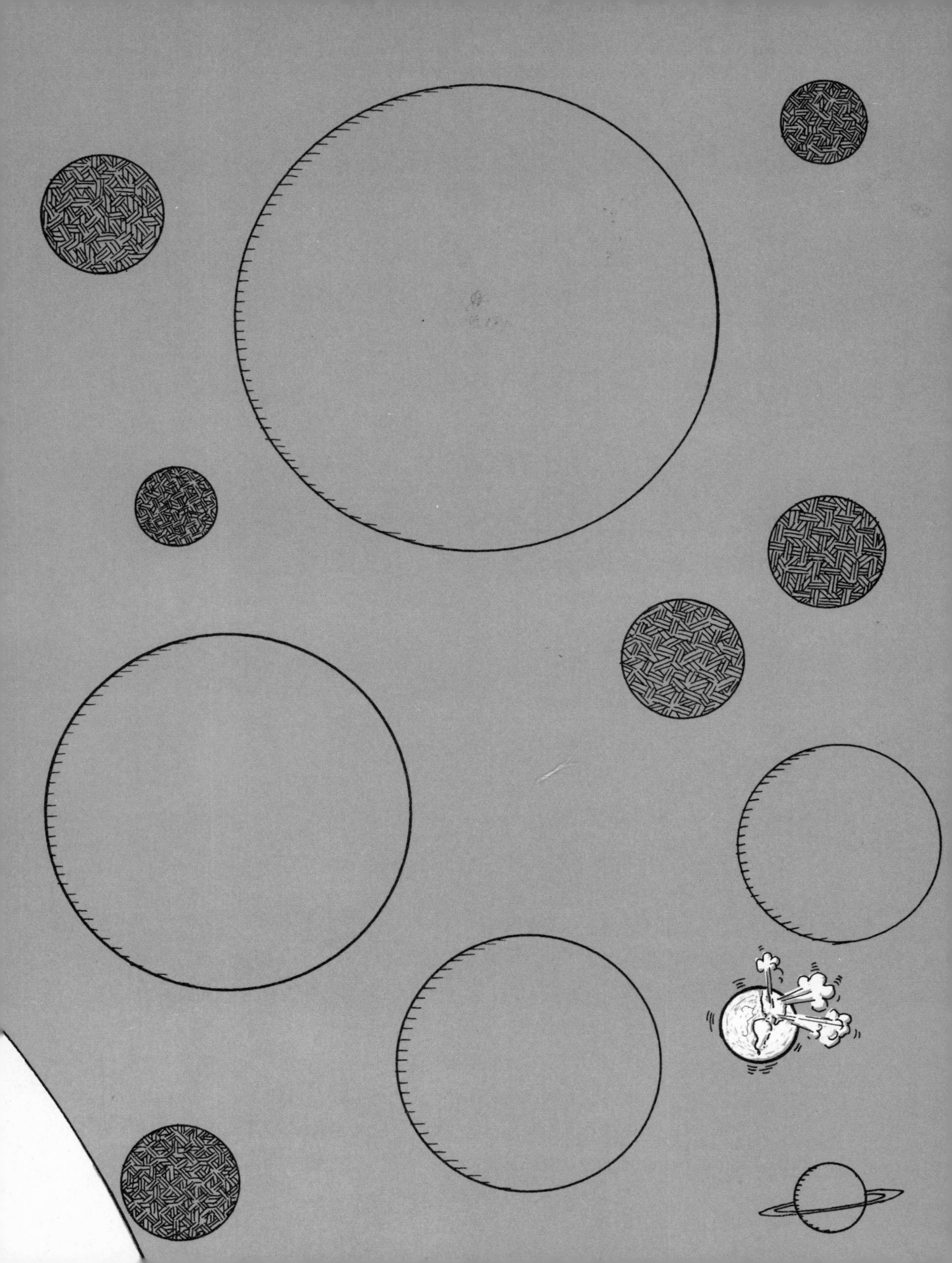

This does not mean science has thrown away Newton's Laws or Maxwell's equations. Their ideas of mechanics and electricity still hold true. Rockets are being built according to Newton's Laws. Radio and television use Maxwell's equations. The Theory of Relativity does not take the place of long-existing laws. It is used for special happenings. It is when objects approach the speed of light, when sub-atomic particles are involved, or when an absolute measurement is needed with respect to reference systems that the classical law set forth by those men need some revision.

UNITED STATES
UNITED STATES

Man has always dreamed of traveling into the past and into the future. This is impossible because of the energy and speed involved. But man likes to dream. As a result of these discoveries a revolution in thought is changing physics into a new science. As you grow older and gain a better understanding of the Theory of Relativity, perhaps you will contribute to giving science a new twist.